199
FAVORITE
BIBLE VERSES
for *Men*

**CHRISTIAN ART
PUBLISHERS**

Contents

What to Do

When I Need ...

Assurance

- 1 -

Since we have a great priest over
the house of God, let us draw near
to God with a sincere heart
in full assurance of faith.

Hebrews 10:21-22

- 2 -

As far as the east is from the west,
so far does He remove our
transgressions from us.

Psalm 103:12 NKJV

- 3 -

The Lord is my light and my
salvation – whom shall I fear? The
Lord is the stronghold of my life –
of whom shall I be afraid?

Psalm 27:1

- 4 -

"I tell you the truth, those
who listen to My message and
believe in God who sent Me have
eternal life. They will never be
condemned for their sins, but they
have already passed from
death into life."

John 5:24 NLT

- 5 -

"I am the LORD, your God, who
takes hold of your right hand and
says to you, 'Do not fear;
I will help you.'"

Isaiah 41:13

*There's no greater comfort
that to remember that you're
living in the center of God's will –
nothing can ever happen to you
without God's permission.*

- Anonymous

Blessed assurance,
Jesus is mine!
Oh, what a foretaste
of glory divine!
Heir of salvation,
purchase of God,
born of the Spirit,
washed in His blood.

– Fanny Crosby

Confidence

- 6 -

Being confident of this very thing,
that He who has begun a good
work in you will complete it until
the day of Jesus Christ.

Philippians 1:6 NKJV

- 7 -

It is better to take refuge in the
LORD than to trust in princes.

Psalm 118:9 NLT

- 8 -

The LORD will be your
confidence and will keep your
foot from being caught.

Proverbs 3:26 ESV

- 9 -

It is the LORD who goes before you. He will be with you; He will not leave you or forsake you. Do not fear or be dismayed.

Deuteronomy 31:8 ESV

- 10 -

So we say with confidence, "The Lord is my helper; I will not be afraid. What can man do to me?"

Hebrews 13:6

Expect great things from God; attempt great things for God.

- William Carey

Oh, how great
peace and quietness
would he possess
who should cut off
all vain anxiety
and place all his
confidence in God.

– Thomas à Kempis

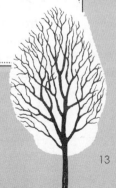

13

- 11 -

Do not let your heart faint,
do not be afraid, and do not
tremble or be terrified; for the
LORD your God is He who goes
with you, to fight for you against
your enemies, to save you.

Deuteronomy 20:3-4 NKJV

- 12 -

If we are faithful to the end, trust-
ing God just as firmly as when we
first believed, we will share in all
that belongs to Christ.

Hebrews 3:14 NLT

- 13 -

God equipped me with
strength and made my way
blameless. He made my feet
like the feet of a deer and set
me secure on the heights.

Psalm 18:32-33 ESV

- 14 -

May our Lord Jesus Christ Himself
and God our Father, who loved us
and by His grace gave us eternal
comfort and a wonderful hope,
comfort you and strengthen you in
every good thing you do and say.

2 Thessalonians 2:16-17 NLT

*We should seize every opportunity
to give encouragement.
Encouragement is oxygen to the soul.*

- George Matthew Adams

Encouragement
costs you nothing
to give, but is
priceless to receive.

– Anonymous

- 15 -

The LORD replied, "My Presence
will go with you, and I will give
you rest."

Exodus 33:14

- 16 -

You hide them in the shelter of
Your presence.

Psalm 31:20 NLT

- 17 -

"Even to your old age and gray
hairs I am He, I am He who will
sustain you. I have made you and
I will carry you; I will sustain you
and I will rescue you."

Isaiah 46:4

- 18 -

"I am with you always, even to the
end of the age."

Matthew 28:20 NKJV

- 19 -

"Behold, I stand at the door
and knock. If anyone hears My
voice and opens the door, I will
come in to him and dine with him,
and he with Me."

Revelation 3:20 NKJV

- 20 -

The LORD is near to all
who call on Him, to all
who call on Him in truth.

Psalm 145:18

*In His love He clothes us, enfolds us
and embraces us; that tender love
completely surrounds us,
never to leave us.*

- Julian of Norwich

What our Lord did was
done with this intent,
and this alone,
that He might be with us
and we with Him.

– Meister Eckhart

Hope

- 21 -

May the God of hope fill you with
all joy and peace in believing, that
you may abound in hope by the
power of the Holy Spirit.

Romans 15:13 NKJV

- 22 -

For You, O Lord, are my hope,
my trust, O LORD, from my youth.

Psalm 71:5 ESV

- 23 -

Let us hold fast the confession
of our hope without wavering,
for He who promised is faithful.

Hebrews 10:23 NKJV

- 24 -

So be strong and courageous,
all you who put your
hope in the LORD!

Psalm 31:24 NLT

- 25 -

Those who hope in the Lord will
renew their strength. They will
soar on wings like eagles; they will
run and not grow weary, they will
walk and not be faint.

Isaiah 40:31

- 26 -

Three things will last forever –
faith, hope, and love.

1 Corinthians 13:13 NLT

Hope is the thing with feathers –
that perches in the soul –
and sings the tunes without the words –
and never stops at all.

- Emily Dickinson

Make no little plans.
They have no magic
to stir men's blood.
Make big plans:
aim high in
hope and work.

– Daniel Hudson Burnham

- 27 -

"My grace is sufficient for you,
for My strength is made
perfect in weakness."

2 Corinthians 12:9 NKJV

- 28 -

He gives power to the faint,
and to him who has no might
He increases strength.

Isaiah 40:29 ESV

- 29 -

My health may fail, and my
spirit may grow weak, but God
remains the strength of my heart;
He is mine forever.

Psalm 73:26 NLT

Strength

- 30 -

For You equipped me with
strength for the battle; You
made those who rise against
me sink under me.

2 Samuel 22:40 ESV

- 31 -

God is my strength and
power, and He makes my way
perfect. He makes my feet like
the feet of deer, and sets
me on my high places.

2 Samuel 22:33-34 NKJV

*It is the mark of weak men
that they break down under unusual
responsibilities, of strong men
that they are developed by them.*

- C. I. Scofield

Do not pray for easy lives.
Pray to be stronger men!
Do not pray for tasks equal to
your powers. Pray for powers
equal to your tasks.
Then the doing of your work
shall be no miracle,
but you shall be a miracle.

– Phillips Brooks

- 32 -

If you need wisdom,
ask our generous God, and
He will give it to you. He will
not rebuke you for asking.

James 1:5 NLT

- 33 -

To the man who pleases Him,
God gives wisdom,
knowledge and happiness.

Ecclesiastes 2:26

- 34 -

The fear of the LORD is the
beginning of wisdom; a good
understanding have all those
who do His commandments.
His praise endures forever.

Psalm 111:10 NKJV

Wisdom

- 35 -

The wisdom from above is first
pure, then peaceable,
gentle, open to reason, full of
mercy and good fruits, impartial
and sincere. And a harvest of
righteousness is sown in peace
by those who make peace.

James 3:17-18 ESV

- 36 -

Wisdom is sweet to your soul.
If you find it, you will have a
bright future, and your hopes
will not be cut short.

Proverbs 24:14 NLT

- 37 -

Oh, the depth of the riches of the
wisdom and knowledge of God!
How unsearchable His judgments,
and His paths beyond tracing out!

Romans 11:33

He is truly wise who
looks upon all earthly
things as folly that
he may gain Christ.

– Thomas à Kempis

What the Bible Says

Concerning ...

Anger

- 38 -

People with understanding control
their anger; a hot temper shows
great foolishness.

Proverbs 14:29 NLT

- 39 -

Refrain from anger and turn
from wrath; do not fret –
it leads only to evil.

Psalm 37:8

- 40 -

If possible, so far as it depends
on you, live peaceably with all.

Romans 12:18 ESV

- 41 -

"In your anger do not sin":
Do not let the sun go down
while you are still angry.

Ephesians 4:26

Anger

- 42 -

Don't befriend angry people or associate with hot-tempered people, or you will learn to be like them and endanger your soul.

Proverbs 22:24-25 NLT

- 43 -

The LORD is compassionate and gracious, slow to anger, abounding in love. He does not treat us as our sins deserve or repay us according to our iniquities.

Psalm 103:8, 10

Anger blows out the lamp of the mind. It's a child's reaction to an adult situation.

- Anonymous

Speak when you are angry
and you will make the best
speech you will ever regret.

– Ambrose Bierce

- 44 -

No discipline is enjoyable while it
is happening – it's painful!
But afterward
there will be a peaceful harvest
of right living for those who
are trained in this way.

Hebrews 12:11 NLT

- 45 -

Blessed is the man whom God
corrects; so do not despise the
discipline of the Almighty.

Job 5:17

- 46 -

Chasten your son while there is
hope, and do not set your heart
on his destruction.

Proverbs 19:18 NKJV

- 47 -

Discipline your children; you'll
be glad you did – they'll turn out
delightful to live with.

Proverbs 29:17 THE MESSAGE

- 48 -

Think about it: Just as a parent
disciplines a child, the LORD your
God disciplines you for your own
good. So obey the commands of
the LORD your God by walking in
His ways and fearing Him.

Deuteronomy 8:5-6 NLT

*The goal of God's discipline
is restoration –
never condemnation.*

- Anonymous

Discipline is the refining
fire by which talent
becomes ability.

– Roy L. Smith

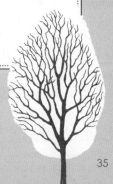

Family

- 49 -

How great is the love the Father
has lavished on us, that we should
be called children of God! And
that is what we are!

1 John 3:1

- 50 -

"Honor your father and mother.
Then you will live a long,
full life in the land the LORD
your God is giving you."

Exodus 20:12 NLT

- 51 -

As a father has compassion
on his children, so the
LORD has compassion
on those who fear Him.

Psalm 103:13

Family

"Whoever does the will of
God, he is My brother and
sister and mother."

Mark 3:35 ESV

Train up a child in the way he
should go, and when he is old
he will not depart from it.

Proverbs 22:6 NKJV

"I will be a Father to you, and you
will be My sons and daughters,
"says the Lord Almighty.

2 Corinthians 6:18

*The most important thing a father can do
for his children is to love their mother.*

- Theodore Hesburgh

The family was ordained by God before He established any other institution, even before He established the church.

– Billy Graham

- 55 -

Trust in the LORD with all your heart, do not depend on your own understanding. Seek His will in all you do, and He will show you which path to take.

Proverbs 3:5-6 NLT

- 56 -

Do not be conformed to this world, but be transformed by the renewing of your mind, that you may prove what is that good and acceptable and perfect will of God.

Romans 12:2 NKJV

- 57 -

The LORD directs the steps of the godly. He delights in every detail of their lives.

Psalm 37:23 NLT

God's Will

- 58 -

The LORD says, "I will guide
you along the best pathway
for your life. I will advise you
and watch over you."

Psalm 32:8 NLT

- 59 -

Give thanks in all circumstances;
for this is the will of God in
Christ Jesus for you.

1 Thessalonians 5:18 ESV

Inside the will of God there is no failure.
Outside the will of God there is no success.

- Bernard Edinger

I find that doing
the will of God
leaves me with
no time for disputing
about His plans.

– George MacDonald

Humility

- 60 -

Humble yourselves in the sight of the Lord, and He will lift you up.

James 4:10 NKJV

- 61 -

"Whoever exalts himself will be humbled, and whoever humbles himself will be exalted."

Matthew 23:12

- 62 -

Don't be selfish; don't try to impress others. Be humble, thinking of others as better than yourselves. Don't look out only for your own interests, but take an interest in others, too.

Philippians 2:3-4 NLT

- 63 -

"Blessed are the meek,
for they will inherit the earth."

Matthew 5:5

- 64 -

The reward for humility and
fear of the LORD is riches
and honor and life.

Proverbs 22:4 ESV

- 65 -

"Whoever humbles himself like
this child is the greatest in the
kingdom of heaven."

Matthew 18:4

*If you plan to build a tall
house of virtues, you must first
lay deep foundations of humility.*

- St. Augustine

Humility is not an ideal,
it is the unconscious
result of the life being
rightly related to God.

– Oswald Chambers

Integrity

- 66 -

As for me, You uphold me
in my integrity, and set me
before Your face forever.

Psalm 41:12 NKJV

- 67 -

May integrity and honesty protect
me, for I put my hope in You.

Psalm 25:21 NLT

- 68 -

May God Himself, the God of
peace, sanctify you through and
through. May your whole spirit,
soul and body be kept blameless
at the coming of our Lord Jesus
Christ. The one who calls you is
faithful and He will do it.

1 Thessalonians 5:23-24

Integrity

- 69 -

Light is shed upon the righteous
and joy on the upright in heart.

Psalm 97:11

- 70 -

The LORD God is a sun and shield;
the LORD will give grace and glory;
no good thing will He withhold
from those who walk uprightly.

Psalm 84:11 NKJV

*Let unswerving integrity
ever be your watchword.*

- Bernard M. Baruch

Integrity: the virtue of
being good without
being watched.

– Anonymous

- 71 -

He who finds a wife finds a
good thing, and obtains
favor from the LORD.

Proverbs 18:22 NKJV

- 72 -

A man will leave his
father and mother
and be united to his wife, and
the two will become one flesh.

Ephesians 5:31

- 73 -

Husbands, live with your wives in
an understanding way, showing
honor to the woman as the weaker
vessel, since they are heirs with
you of the grace of life, so that
your prayers may not be hindered.

1 Peter 3:7 ESV

Marriage

- 74 -

May your fountain be blessed,
and may you rejoice in the
wife of your youth.

Proverbs 5:18

- 75 -

Let the husband render to his wife
the affection due her, and likewise
also the wife to her husband.

1 Corinthians 7:3 NKJV

*Marriage should be a duet –
when one sings, the other claps.*

- Joe Murray

In a successful marriage, there is no such thing as one's way. There is only the way of both, only the bumpy, dusty, difficult, but always mutual path.

– Phyllis McGinley

- 76 -

"No one can serve two masters.
Either he will hate the one and
love the other, or he will be
devoted to the one and despise
the other. You cannot serve
both God and money."

Matthew 6:24

- 77 -

"Seek the Kingdom of God
above all else, and live
righteously, and He will give
you everything you need."

Matthew 6:33 NLT

- 78 -

"Where your treasure is,
there your heart will be also."

Matthew 6:21

- 79 -

"If anyone would come after
Me, let him deny himself and take
up his cross and follow Me.
For whoever would save his life
will lose it, but whoever loses his
life for My sake will find it.
For what will it profit a man if
he gains the whole world and
forfeits his life? Or what shall a
man give in return for his life?"

Matthew 16:24-26 ESV

*Lord, we don't mind who is second
as long as Thou art first.*

- W. E. Sangster

You can't get second things
by putting them first;
you can get second things
only by putting
first things first.

– C. S. Lewis

Wealth

- 80 -

It is a good thing to receive wealth
from God and the good health
to enjoy it. To enjoy your work
and accept your lot in life – that is
indeed a gift from God.

Ecclesiastes 5:19 NLT

- 81 -

"Seek first the kingdom
of God and His righteousness,
and all these things shall
be added to you."

Matthew 6:33 NKJV

- 82 -

I have learned how to be
content with whatever I have.
I have learned the secret of
living in every situation.

Philippians 4:11-12 NLT

Wealth

- 83 -

Keep your life free
from love of money,
and be content with
what you have.

Hebrews 13:5 ESV

- 84 -

Whoever trusts in his riches
will fall, but the righteous
will thrive like a green leaf.

Proverbs 11:28

*If you want to feel rich, just count all the
things you have that money can't buy.*

- Anonymous

The happiest of people
don't necessarily have
the best of everything.
They just make the
best of everything.

– Roy O. Disney

Rely on

God for . . .

- 85 -

Many are the plans in the mind
of a man, but it is the purpose
of the Lord that will stand.

Proverbs 19:21 ESV

- 86 -

"For I know the plans I have
for you," declares the Lord,
"plans to prosper you and not
to harm you, plans to give
you hope and a future."

Jeremiah 29:11

- 87 -

The Lord will fulfill His purpose for
me; Your steadfast love, O Lord,
endures forever. Do not forsake
the work of Your hands.

Psalm 138:8 ESV

- 88 -

Consider the blameless,
observe the upright; there is a
future for the man of peace.

Psalm 37:37

- 89 -

Don't brag about tomorrow,
since you don't know what
the day will bring.

Proverbs 27:1 NLT

*The wise man must remember
that while he is a descendant of the past,
he is a parent of the future.*

- Herbert Spencer

The future has
several names.
For the weak,
it is the impossible.
For the fainthearted,
it is the unknown.
For the thoughtful
and valiant,
it is the ideal.

– Victor Hugo

- 90 -

This God is our God for ever
and ever; He will be our
guide even to the end.

Psalm 48:14

- 91 -

A man's heart plans his way,
but the LORD directs his steps.

Proverbs 16:9 NKJV

- 92 -

He will not let your foot slip – He
who watches over you will not
slumber; indeed, He who
watches over Israel will neither
slumber nor sleep. The LORD
watches over you – the LORD is
your shade at your right hand;
the sun will not harm you by day,
nor the moon by night.

Psalm 121:3-6

- 93 -

The LORD says, "I will guide
you along the best pathway
for your life. I will advise you
and watch over you."

Psalm 32:8 NLT

- 94 -

The steps of a man are
established by the LORD,
when He delights in his way.

Psalm 37:23 ESV

- 95 -

Show me Your ways, O LORD;
teach me Your paths. Lead me
in Your truth and teach me, for
You are the God of my salvation;
on You I wait all the day.

Psalm 25:4-5 NKJV

I am satisfied that
when the Almighty wants me
to do or not to do
any particular thing,
He finds a way
of letting me know.

– Abraham Lincoln

- 96 -

I will lift up my eyes to the hills –
from whence comes my help? My
help comes from the LORD, who
made heaven and earth.

Psalm 121:1-2 NKJV

- 97 -

God is our refuge and strength, an
ever-present help in trouble.

Psalm 46:1

- 98 -

The LORD is my strength and my
shield; in Him my heart trusts, and
I am helped; my heart exults, and
with my song I give thanks to Him.

Psalm 28:7 ESV

- 99 -

The LORD is good, a stronghold in
the day of trouble; and He knows
those who trust in Him.

Nahum 1:7 NKJV

God, who foresaw
your tribulation, has
specially armed you to
go through it, not without
pain but without stain.

– C. S. Lewis

Patience

- 100 -

Wait for the LORD; be strong and take heart and wait for the LORD.

Psalm 27:14

- 101 -

You also be patient. Establish your hearts, for the coming of the Lord is at hand.

James 5:8 NKJV

- 102 -

The Lord isn't really being slow about His promise, as some people think. No, He is being patient for our sake. He does not want anyone to be destroyed, but wants everyone to repent.

2 Peter 3:9 NLT

Patience

- 103 -

I waited patiently for the LORD; He
inclined to me and heard my cry.

Psalm 40:1 ESV

- 104 -

Since God chose you to be
the holy people He loves, you
must clothe yourselves with
tenderhearted mercy, kindness,
humility, gentleness,
and patience.

Colossians 3:12 NLT

Patience with others is love.
Patience with self is hope.
Patience with God is faith.

- Adel Bestavros

This would be a fine world
if all men showed as
much patience all the time
as they do while they're
waiting for the fish to bite.

– Vaughn Monroe

- 105 -

"I am leaving you with a gift –
peace of mind and heart.
And the peace I give is a gift
the world cannot give. So
don't be troubled or afraid."

John 14:27 NLT

- 106 -

I will both lie down in peace,
and sleep; for You alone, O LORD,
make me dwell in safety.

Psalm 4:8 NKJV

- 107 -

You will keep in perfect peace
all who trust in You, all whose
thoughts are fixed on You!

Isaiah 26:3 NLT

- 108 -

May the Lord of peace Himself
give you His peace at all
times and in every situation.
The Lord be with you all.

2 Thessalonians 3:16 NLT

- 109 -

Let the peace of Christ rule in your
hearts, since as members of one
body you were called to peace.
And be thankful.

Colossians 3:15

*Peace is the deliberate adjustment
of my life to the will of God.*

- Anonymous

All things that
speak of heaven
speak of peace.

– Philip J. Bailey

- 110 -

"Your Father knows the
things you have need of
before you ask Him."

Matthew 6:8 NKJV

- 111 -

My God will meet all your
needs according to His glorious
riches in Christ Jesus.

Philippians 4:19

- 112 -

His divine power has granted to
us all things that pertain to life and
godliness, through the knowledge
of Him who called us to His own
glory and excellence, by which
He has granted to us His precious
and very great promises.

2 Peter 1:3-4 ESV

- 113 -

Don't forget to do good and to
share with those in need. These
are the sacrifices that please God.

Hebrews 13:16 NLT

- 114 -

He will give grass in your fields for
your livestock, and you shall eat
and be full.

Deuteronomy 11:15 ESV

*To believe that He will preserve us is,
indeed, a means of preservation.*

- John Owen

If God sends us
on stony paths,
He will provide us
with strong shoes.

– Alexander MacLaren

Success

- 115 -

Commit to the LORD whatever you
do, and your plans will succeed.

Proverbs 16:3

- 116 -

"I know the thoughts I think
toward you," says the LORD,
"thoughts of peace and
not of evil, to give you a
future and a hope."

Jeremiah 29:11 NKJV

- 117 -

Whatever you do, work at it with
all your heart, as working for the
Lord, not for men, since you know
that you will receive an inheritance
from the Lord as a reward.

Colossians 3:23-24

- 118 -

It is not that we think we are
qualified to do anything
on our own. Our qualification
comes from God.

2 Corinthians 3:5 NLT

- 119 -

May the LORD give you the desire
of your heart and make all your
plans succeed.

Psalm 20:4

*The key to happiness is having
dreams. The key to success is
making your dreams come true.*

- Anonymous

God Freely

Gives ...

- 120 -

Praise be to the God and Father
of our Lord Jesus Christ, the
Father of compassion and the
God of all comfort, who comforts
us in all our troubles.

2 Corinthians 1:3-4

- 121 -

"Blessed are those who mourn,
for they shall be comforted."

Matthew 5:4 NKJV

- 122 -

"As a mother comforts her
child, so will I comfort you;
and you will be comforted."

Isaiah 66:13

- 123 -

"I will not leave you comfortless:
I will come to you."

John 14:18 KJV

- 124 -

Cast your burden on the LORD,
and He shall sustain you; He shall
never permit the righteous to be
moved.

Psalm 55:22 NKJV

*God often comforts us, not by changing
the circumstances of our lives, but by
changing our attitude toward them.*

- S. H. B. Masterman

God does not
comfort us to
make us comfortable,
but to make
us comforters.

– J. H. Jowett

- 125 -

Be of good courage, and He
shall strengthen your heart,
all you who hope in the LORD.

Psalm 31:24 NKJV

- 126 -

"Be strong and courageous. Do
not be frightened, and do not be
dismayed, for the LORD your God
is with you wherever you go."

Joshua 1:9 ESV

- 127 -

In Your strength I can
crush an army; with my
God I can scale any wall.

Psalm 18:29 NLT

Courage

- 128 -

"Fear not, for I am with you; be not dismayed, for I am your God; I will strengthen you, I will help you, I will uphold you with My righteous right hand."

Isaiah 41:10 ESV

- 129 -

Having hope will give you courage. You will be protected and will rest in safety.

Job 11:18 NLT

Courage is not the absence of fear, but rather the judgment that something else is more important than fear.

- Ambrose Redmoon

Courage is an
inner resolution to
go forward in spite
of obstacles and
frightening situations.

– Martin Luther King, Jr.

83

Forgiveness

- 130 -

If we confess our sins, He is
faithful and just to forgive us
our sins and to cleanse us
from all unrighteousness.

1 John 1:9 ESV

- 131 -

"I will forgive their wickedness,
and I will never again
remember their sins."

Hebrews 8:12 NLT

- 132 -

"Come now, let us reason
together," says the LORD.
"Though your sins are like scarlet,
they shall be as white as snow;
though they are red as crimson,
they shall be like wool."

Isaiah 1:18

- 133 -

"If My people who are called by
My name will humble themselves,
and pray and seek My face, and
turn from their wicked ways, then
I will hear from heaven,
and will forgive their
sin and heal their land."

2 Chronicles 7:14 NKJV

- 134 -

"When you stand praying,
if you hold anything against
anyone, forgive him, so
that your Father in heaven
may forgive you your sins."

Mark 11:25

We win by tenderness;
we conquer by forgiveness.

- Frederick W. Robertson

We have a free, full, final, forever forgiveness in the atoning work of Christ.

– J. Sidlow Baxter

Grace

- 135 -

"My grace is all you need. My power works best in weakness."

2 Corinthians 12:9 NLT

- 136 -

Where sin increased, grace increased all the more.

Romans 5:20

- 137 -

God is able to make all grace abound toward you, that you, always having all sufficiency in all things, may have an abundance for every good work.

2 Corinthians 9:8 NKJV

- 138 -

God opposes the proud but gives
grace to the humble.

James 4:6 ESV

- 139 -

You know the grace of our Lord
Jesus Christ, that though He was
rich, yet for your sakes He became
poor, so that you through His
poverty might become rich.

2 Corinthians 8:9

Grace is but glory begun,
and glory is but grace perfected.

- Jonathan Edwards

The word grace is
unquestionably the most
significant single word
in the Bible.

– Ilion T. Jones

Love

- 140 -

For God so loved the world that
He gave His one and only Son,
that whoever believes in Him shall
not perish but have eternal life.

John 3:16

- 141 -

Show deep love for each other, for
love covers a multitude of sins.

1 Peter 4:8 NLT

- 142 -

Love is patient, love is kind. It
does not envy, it does not boast,
it is not proud. It is not rude, it is
not self-seeking, it is not easily
angered, it keeps no record of
wrongs. Love does not delight
in evil but rejoices with the truth.
It always protects, always trusts,
always hopes, always perseveres.
Love never fails.

1 Corinthians 13:4-8

- 143 -

"A new command I give you:
Love one another. As I have
loved you, so you must
love one another. By this
all men will know that you are My
disciples, if you love one another."

John 13:34-35

- 144 -

I am persuaded that neither
death nor life, nor angels nor
principalities nor powers, nor
things present nor things to come,
nor height nor depth, nor any
other created thing, shall
be able to separate us from
the love of God which is in
Christ Jesus our Lord.

Romans 8:38-39 NKJV

Human love fails and
will always fail.
God's love never fails.

– Corrie ten Boom

Mercy

- 145 -

The LORD is gracious and full of compassion, slow to anger and great in mercy. The LORD is good to all, and His tender mercies are over all His works.

Psalm 145:8-9 NKJV

- 146 -

Because of God's tender mercy, the morning light from heaven is about to break upon us, to give light to those who sit in darkness and in the shadow of death, and to guide us to the path of peace.

Luke 1:78-79 NLT

- 147 -

To the Lord our God belong mercy and forgiveness.

Daniel 9:9 ESV

- 148 -

God saved us, not because of
the righteous things we had done,
but because of His mercy.

Titus 3:5 NLT

- 149 -

"Blessed are the merciful,
for they will be shown mercy.
Blessed are the pure in heart,
for they will see God."

Matthew 5:7-8

Two words of mercy set a man free:
forgive and you will be forgiven,
and give and you will receive.

- St. Augustine

Teach me to feel
another's woe,
to hide the fault I see;
That mercy I to
others show,
that mercy
show to me.

– Alexander Pope

Self-Control

- 150 -

Guard your heart above
all else, for it determines
the course of your life.

Proverbs 4:23 NLT

- 151 -

God gave us a spirit not
of fear but of power and
love and self-control.

2 Timothy 1:7 ESV

- 152 -

So think clearly and exercise
self-control. Look forward to
the gracious salvation that
will come to you when Jesus
Christ is revealed to the world.
So you must live as God's
obedient children. Don't slip back
into your old ways of living to
satisfy your own desires.

1 Peter 1:13-14 NLT

- 153 -

Make every effort to add to your faith goodness; and to goodness, knowledge; and to knowledge, self-control; and to self-control, perseverance; and to perseverance, godliness; and to godliness, brotherly kindness; and to brotherly kindness, love. For if you possess these qualities in increasing measure, they will keep you from being ineffective and unproductive in your knowledge of our Lord Jesus Christ.

2 Peter 1:5-8

There has never been, and cannot be, a good life, without self-control.

Self-control is more
often called for
than self-expression.

– William M. Comfort

98

God Wants

You to …

Be Bold

- 154 -

So we may boldly say:
"The LORD is my helper; I will not
fear. What can man do to me?"

Hebrews 13:6 NKJV

- 155 -

Wait for the LORD; be strong,
and let your heart take
courage; wait for the LORD!

Psalm 27:14 ESV

- 156 -

"Be strong and courageous.
Do not be terrified; do not be
discouraged, for the LORD
your God will be with you
wherever you go."

Joshua 1:9

Be Bold

"Fear not, for I am with you; be not dismayed, for I am your God. I will strengthen you, yes, I will help you, I will uphold you with My righteous right hand."

Isaiah 41:10 NKJV

- 158 -

Overwhelming victory is ours through Christ, who loved us.

Romans 8:37 NLT

*I am only one, but still I am one.
I cannot do everything,
but still I can do something;
I will not refuse to do the
something I can do.*

- Helen Keller

Whatever you can do,
or dream you can, begin it.
Boldness has genius,
power, and magic in it.

- Johann von Goethe

Be Kind

- 159 -

But the Holy Spirit produces
this kind of fruit in our lives:
love, joy, peace, patience,
kindness, goodness, faithfulness,
gentleness, and self-control.

Galatians 5:22-23 NLT

- 160 -

Instead be kind to one other,
tenderhearted, forgiving
one another, as God through
Christ forgave you.

Ephesians 4:32 NLT

- 161 -

Your kindness will reward you,
but your cruelty will destroy you.

Proverbs 11:17 NLT

Be Kind

- 162 -

Make sure that nobody pays
back wrong for wrong, but
always try to be kind to each
other and to everyone else.

1 Thessalonians 5:15

- 163 -

Whoever is kind to the
needy honors God.

Proverbs 14:31

*The person who sows seeds of kindness
enjoys a perpetual harvest.*

- Anonymous

Kindness makes a fellow
feel good whether it's being
done to him or by him.

– Frank A. Clark

- 164 -

"Whoever wants to become great among you must be your servant, and whoever wants to be first must be slave of all. For even the Son of Man did not come to be served, but to serve, and to give His life as a ransom for many."

Mark 10:43-45

- 165 -

Let no one despise you for your youth, but set the believers an example in speech, in conduct, in love, in faith, in purity. Persist in this, for by so doing you will save both yourself and your hearers.

1 Timothy 4:12, 16 ESV

- 166 -

Work hard and become a leader.

Proverbs 12:24 NLT

Be a Leader

- 167 -

He must manage his own family
well and see that his children
obey him with proper respect.

1 Timothy 3:4

- 168 -

He has told you, O man, what is
good; and what does the LORD
require of you but to do justice,
and to love kindness, and to walk
humbly with your God?

Micah 6:8 ESV

- 169 -

A good leader motivates,
doesn't mislead, doesn't
exploit. GOD cares about
honesty in the workplace; your
business is His business.

Proverbs 16:10-11 THE MESSAGE

Leaders who develop
people, add.
Leaders who develop
leaders, multiply.

– John C. Maxwell

- 170 -

Do not be rash with your mouth,
and let not your heart utter
anything hastily before God.
For God is in heaven,
and you on earth; therefore
let your words be few.

Ecclesiastes 5:2 NKJV

- 171 -

Don't call attention to yourself;
let others do that for you.

Proverbs 27:2 THE MESSAGE

- 172 -

God gives us more grace.
That is why Scripture says:
"God opposes the proud but
gives grace to the humble."

James 4:6

Be Modest

- 173 -

Do not boast about tomorrow,
for you do not know
what a day may bring.

Proverbs 27:1 ESV

- 174 -

Pride ends in humiliation,
while humility brings honor.

Proverbs 29:23 NLT

Great modesty often hides great merit.

- Benjamin Franklin

The Holy Spirit finds
modesty so rare that
He takes care to record it.
Say much of what the
Lord has done for you,
but say little of what you
have done for the Lord.
Do not utter a
self-glorifying sentence!

– Charles H. Spurgeon

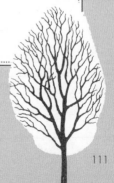

- 175 -

The earnest prayer of a righteous
person has great power and
produces wonderful results.

James 5:16 NLT

- 176 -

The LORD is near to all who call
on Him, to all who call on Him in
truth. He fulfills the desires
of those who fear Him; He hears
their cry and saves them.

Psalm 145:18-19

- 177 -

"Whatever you ask in prayer, you
will receive, if you have faith."

Matthew 21:22 ESV

- 178 -

"But when you pray, go into your
room, close the door and pray to
your Father, who is unseen. Then
your Father, who sees what is
done in secret, will reward you."

Matthew 6:6

- 179 -

"I say to you, whatever things
you ask when you pray,
believe that you receive them,
and you will have them."

Mark 11:24 NKJV

Prayer should not be regarded as a duty
which must be performed, but rather as a
privilege to be enjoyed, a rare delight that
is always revealing some new beauty.

- E. M. Bounds

The men who have
done the most
for God in this
world have been early
on their knees.

– E. M. Bounds

- 180 -

Blessed is the man who endures
temptation; for when he has been
approved, he will receive the
crown of life which the Lord has
promised to those who love Him.

James 1:12 NKJV

- 181 -

Therefore, my beloved brothers,
be steadfast, immovable, always
abounding in the work of the
Lord, knowing that in the Lord
your labor is not in vain.

1 Corinthians 15:58 ESV

- 182 -

"The one who endures
to the end will be saved."

Matthew 24:13 NLT

- 183 -

Not only so, but we also rejoice
in our sufferings, because we
know that suffering produces
perseverance; perseverance,
character; and character, hope.
And hope does not disappoint us,
because God has poured out His
love into our hearts by the Holy
Spirit, whom He has given us.

Romans 5:3-5

- 184 -

"Because you have obeyed My
command to persevere, I will
protect you from the great time
of testing that will come upon the
whole world to test those who
belong to this world."

Revelation 3:10 NLT

By perseverance the snail reached the ark.

- Charles H. Spurgeon

Our motto must continue
to be perseverance.
And ultimately I trust
the Almighty will crown
our efforts with success.

– William Wilberforce

117

- 185 -

Do nothing out of selfish
ambition or vain conceit,
but in humility consider others
better than yourselves.

Philippians 2:3

- 186 -

You, dear friends,
must build each other
up in your most holy faith,
pray in the power
of the Holy Spirit.

Jude 20 NLT

- 187 -

Honor your father and
your mother, so that you may
live long in the land the
LORD your God is giving you.

Exodus 20:12

- 188 -

Pay to all what is owed to them:
taxes to whom taxes are owed,
revenue to whom revenue is
owed, respect to whom
respect is owed, honor
to whom honor is owed.

Romans 13:7 ESV

- 189 -

Show proper respect to everyone:
love the brotherhood of believers.

1 Peter 2:17

He that respects not is not respected.

- George Herbert

Without respect,
love cannot go
far or rise high:
it is an angel with
but one wing.

– Alexandre Dumas

Work

- 190 -

Whatever you do, work at it with
all your heart, as working for the
Lord, not for men, since you know
that you will receive an inheritance
from the Lord as a reward. It is the
Lord Christ you are serving.

Colossians 3:23-24

- 191 -

His lord said to him, "Well done,
good and faithful servant; you
have been faithful over a few
things, I will make you ruler
over many things. Enter into
the joy of your lord."

Matthew 25:23 NKJV

- 192 -

Do your best to present yourself
to God as one approved, a worker
who has no need to be ashamed,
rightly handling the word of truth.

2 Timothy 2:15 ESV

Work

- 193 -

The LORD will open the heavens, the storehouse of His bounty, to send rain on your land in season and to bless all the work of your hands.

Deuteronomy 28:12

- 194 -

"Take My yoke upon you, and learn from Me, for I am gentle and lowly in heart, and you will find rest for your souls. For My yoke is easy, and My burden is light."

Matthew 11:29-30 ESV

When work is a pleasure; life is a joy.

- Maxim Gorky

For anything worth having
one must pay the price;
and the price is always work,
patience, love, self-sacrifice.

– John Burroughs

Worship

- 195 -

"God is spirit, and His
worshipers must worship
in spirit and in truth."

John 4:24

- 196 -

Honor the LORD for the glory of
His name. Worship the LORD in
the splendor of His holiness.

Psalm 29:2 NLT

- 197 -

So here's what I want you to do,
God helping you: Take your
everyday, ordinary life – your
sleeping, eating, going-to-work,
and walking-around life – and
place it before God as an offering.
Embracing what God does
for you is the best thing
you can do for Him.

Romans 12:1 THE MESSAGE

Worship

- 198 -

I praise You because I am
fearfully and wonderfully made;
Your works are wonderful,
I know that full well.

Psalm 139:14

- 199 -

For great is the LORD, and greatly
to be praised, and He is to be
held in awe above all gods.

1 Chronicles 16:25 ESV

*The more a man bows his knee before
God, the straighter he stands before men.*

- Anonymous

It is only when men
begin to worship
that they begin to grow.

– Calvin Coolidge

126